FOOTSTEPS TO FREEDOM

THE UNDERGROUND RAILROAD

FREE AT LAST?

CLAIRE O'NEAL

PURPLE TOAD
PUBLISHING

FOOTSTEPS TO
FREEDOM
THE UNDERGROUND RAILROAD

FAMOUS FIGHTERS by Wayne L. Wilson
FREE AT LAST? by Claire O'Neal
THE NEED FOR FLIGHT by Claire O'Neal
GOING UNDERGROUND by Amie Jane Leavitt

Copyright © 2016 by Purple Toad Publishing, Inc.

PUBLISHER'S NOTE

The *Footsteps to Freedom: The Underground Railroad* series covers slavery and racism in United States history. Some of the events told in this series may be disturbing to young readers. The data in this book has been researched in depth, and to the best of our knowledge is factual. Although every measure is taken to give an accurate account, Purple Toad Publishing makes no warranty of the accuracy of the information and is not liable for damages caused by inaccuracies.

ABOUT THE AUTHOR

Claire O'Neal has written over thirty books for children. She holds degrees in English and Biology from Indiana University, and a PhD in Chemistry from the University of Washington. She loves reading and writing, and especially learning more about history and culture. Claire lives with her husband and two sons in Delaware.

Printing   1   2   3   4   5   6   7   8   9

Publisher's Cataloging-in-Publication Data
O'Neal, Clare.
   Free at last / written by Clare O'Neal.
      p. cm.
Includes bibliographic references and index.
ISBN 9781624692154
1. Underground Railroad--Juvenile literature. 2. Antislavery movements—United States—Juvenile literature. I. Series: Footsteps to Freedom The Underground Railroad.
 E450 2016
 973.7115
Library of Congress Control Number: 2015941831

ebook ISBN: 9781624692161

CONTENTS

FREE AT LAST!

June 19, 1865, was another scorching summer Monday in Galveston, Texas. A crowd of slaves murmured with hope and excitement. Major General John Granger had traveled to Galveston all the way from Washington, D.C. He brought amazing news, news that the state of Texas was the last to hear: *"The people of Texas are informed that in accordance with a Proclamation from the Executive of the United States, all slaves are free."*

At that moment, the last black slaves in the United States knew that they were slaves no more. The newly freed people shouted with joy. They stomped and danced and jumped and ran. They shed their cares and fear like heavy chains, dropping their hoes and shovels and walking away from their lives of sadness and pain. They cried and sang in sweet harmony:

Free at last, free at last,
Thank God almighty, we are free at last!

A Union soldier shares the good news of freedom with a group of slaves.

Nearly 250 years had passed since the arrival of the first slave to America on a Dutch ship in 1619. When the 13th Amendment passed on January 31, 1865, slavery had finally become illegal in the United States. It took six months for the news to spread.

But what did their freedom *mean*? The former slaves were not sure. They began a blank future empty-handed, with no land and little money. Where would they live? How would they feed their families? Would there be jobs for them? The law once forbade slaves from reading or writing. Would they learn now? Would there be schools for them?

And what, exactly, did the newly freed slaves *want*? Garrison Frazier, a 67-year-old minister and former slave, put it simply for Union General William T. Sherman: "The way we can best take care of ourselves, is to have land, and turn it and till it by our own labor . . . and we can soon maintain ourselves."[1]

General William T. Sherman

Frazier dreamed the American Dream—in which ordinary people could own land, and with it, make their own destiny. General Sherman understood. He issued Special Field Order #15, declaring that 400,000 acres of shoreline from Charleston, South Carolina, to northeast Florida would belong to former slaves. Each black family could have 40 acres. Sherman even told his army to loan mules to the freedmen to help them farm.

Sherman's order began the long and slow process of helping whites and blacks rebuild the American South, a time known as Reconstruction. The Civil War had ended in 1865 with Southern whites hurt and angry. Their cause was lost; the slaves were now freed. In their eyes, what should have been a quick family feud with their Northern cousins had turned into a bloody

Civil War. Many white sons came home either injured or not at all. Southern lands lay in ruin. Whole towns still smoldered, destroyed in the fighting, with homes and businesses burned out or knocked down, fields trampled.

The U.S. Congress created the Freedmen's Bureau to help repair the broken South. First, the Freedmen's Bureau fed the hungry. Between 1865 and 1877, the Bureau delivered over 21 million rations of bread, pork, and beans, as well as wood or coal for cooking, to blacks and whites alike.[2]

Next, the Freedmen's Bureau set up free schools for black children across the South. Many former slave parents

A war-weary Confederate soldier finds his house destroyed.

Newly freed slaves wait in line for their rations from the Freedmen's Bureau.

sat in school beside their children. By 1870, 250,000 students were attending schools sponsored by the Freedmen's Bureau.[3]

Finally, the Bureau stationed Union soldiers in the South to keep the peace. Whites still simmered with the rage of defeat. Blacks, the soldiers feared, might seek revenge against their former masters.

U.S. soldiers served an important mission in the Freedmen's Bureau: protecting blacks from angry whites, and vice versa.

Rebuilding a society built on slavery was expensive and took longer than expected. People in the North grew weary of using their tax dollars to pay for Reconstruction. New factories popped up across the busy North, bringing jobs and technology to the cities. Washington, D.C., eagerly turned its eye to the dollar signs of business, and away from the complicated work still needed by the South. With Abraham Lincoln shot dead by a Southerner in 1865, his allies lost ground. Congress dismantled the Freedmen's Bureau in 1877 and ordered Union troops to return home. White Southern lawmakers assured Congress that they could handle rebuilding on their own.

But Southern whites had no intention of sharing their land, let alone their government, taxes, or even schools, with people who not long ago had been under their complete control. As South Carolina governor Benjamin Perry declared, "This is the white man's government!"[4] Wealthy white Southerners had built up their fortunes on the backbreaking work of slaves. They still had enough money and power to bend the law to their will.

It wasn't long before the black families who had been given 40 acres and a mule were commanded to hand the land back to the whites. "You take them from us who are true, always true to the Government!" shouted a black protester, a voice for blacks everywhere. "That is not right!"[5]

Slavery was over, but whites remained in power. And across the South, whites were determined to keep blacks less than equal under state law.

Jobs for Free Blacks

When the 13th Amendment was ratified, nearly 500,000 free blacks already lived in cities and small farms across the United States. Most lived in the slave states of Maryland and Virginia.[6] They earned their living much as poor whites did, as maids, paid servants, sailors, or skilled craftsmen like blacksmiths and shoemakers. Some free blacks owned small farms, and some even owned slaves. These free men and women paid taxes, but they often could not vote or go to school. Free blacks had to have jobs, or they could be arrested and sold into slavery as state property.

A new law passed in 1939 provided federal money to sharecroppers. Instead, thousands of sharecroppers found themselves homeless, as landlords kicked them off the land and kept the payments for themselves.

The 4 million newly freed slaves vastly outnumbered the already free blacks. They needed jobs fast to keep their families from starving. Meanwhile, plantation owners suddenly had many job openings for sharecroppers—laborers to plant and harvest cotton and tobacco for them. To his ex-slaves, Old Master now promised a share in the cash he made selling crops at harvest time. But as former slave Ulrich Evans put it, "We always get through with fine big crops and owed the white man more than when we started the crop and got to stay to pay the debt."[7] Old Master demanded his money back at the end of the season, in rent for the land, for farming equipment, for the cost of seeds and sometimes food, housing, and clothes. Blacks rarely earned any money at all. Sharecropping became a new way to keep blacks enslaved.

CHAPTER 2

WHITES ONLY, COLOREDS ONLY

Homer Plessy bought a first-class ticket to ride the East Louisiana Railroad in 1892, looking to start trouble. The 30-year-old shoemaker took a seat in the carriage that said WHITES ONLY. Plessy's pale skin certainly made him look white. But because his great-grandmother had been born in Africa, the law declared that Plessy was black.

Louisiana's Separate Car Act of 1890 stated that, for the comfort of travelers, train companies must provide "separate railway carriages for the white and colored races".[1] Plessy argued that, though the Separate Car Act was the law in Louisiana, it was actually against U.S. law. It violated Plessy's rights as a citizen.

Soon after the Civil War ended, Congress had passed many Reconstruction Acts to protect blacks like Plessy. In 1868, the 14th Amendment made it illegal for any state to make special laws that take away a person's rights. The 15th Amendment became law in 1870, protecting the right of blacks and former slaves to vote. Southern states

This illustration shows a darker skinned Homer Plessy about to be kicked off a Louisiana first-class train car for being black.

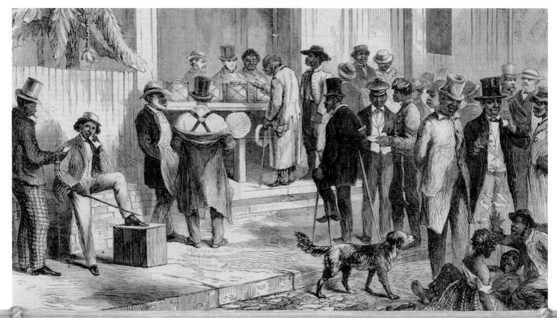

The 15th Amendment gave blacks the right to vote, but many Southern states passed laws that forced blacks to pay a tax or take special tests before they could cast a ballot.

grumbled but were forced to agree with the amendments. If they did not, they would not be admitted to Congress.

Homer Plessy knew the Separate Car Act was unfair. Southern states had crafted many such "Jim Crow" laws, a nickname for laws designed to keep whites in charge and blacks out of the picture. In 1875, Tennessee passed a law that allowed hotels, railroads, and restaurants to refuse black customers. Other states soon followed. By 1885, black children could not attend school with white children in any Southern state. (Many Northern states had similar laws.)

Plessy counted on the Supreme Court to put blacks back on equal footing. But on May 18, 1896, the Court ruled 7-1 against Plessy. Laws cannot prevent people from seeing black and white, Justice Henry Billings Brown wrote. "If one race be inferior to the other socially, the Constitution of the United States cannot put them upon the same plane."[2] In other words, even though blacks and whites were *equal*, laws could still keep them *separate*. Everywhere across the South, Jim Crow became the law of the land.[3]

- *No white shall marry a colored person. (Nearly all states)*
- *Separate soda machines must be provided for whites and colored persons. (Mississippi)*
- *Bathrooms for coloreds shall be separate from the white race. (Oklahoma)*
- *Telephone companies must maintain separate booths for white and colored patrons. (Oklahoma)*
- *Whites and colored persons may not play checkers or dominoes together. (Georgia)*
- *Public parks and playgrounds must be kept separate. (Kentucky)*
- *Colored persons must be out of public spaces by 10:00 each evening. (Alabama)*
- *Circuses must provide separate ticket booths, one serving whites and one serving colored patrons, which must be kept at least 25 feet apart. (Louisiana)*
- *The coffins containing the remains of colored persons may not be buried in white cemeteries. (Georgia)*
- *Colored barbers may not cut the hair of white girls or women. (Georgia)*
- *Races must be kept separate in prisons. (Kentucky)*
- *School textbooks for colored students must not be stored with textbooks for white students. (Florida)*

A sign in a train station marked the separate waiting room for blacks.

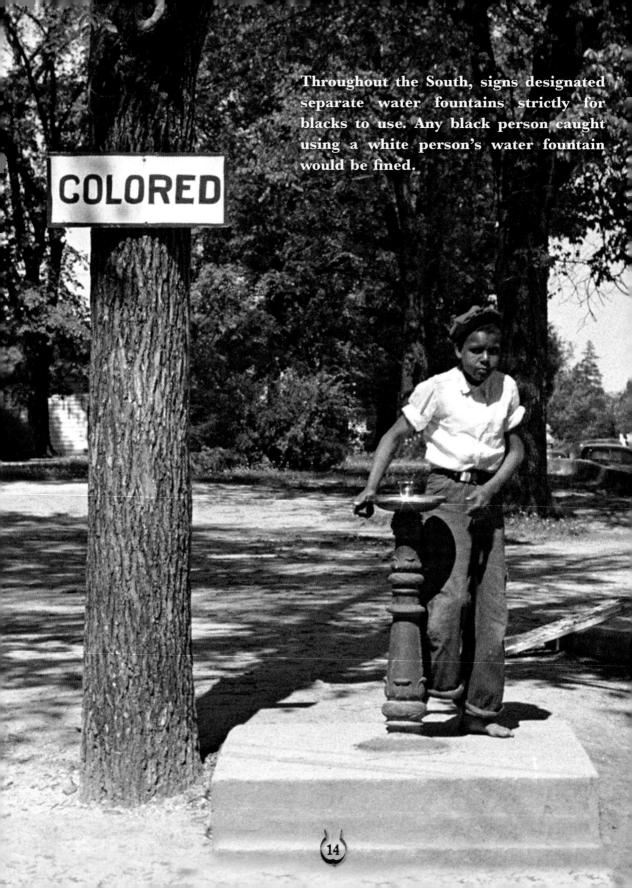

Throughout the South, signs designated separate water fountains strictly for blacks to use. Any black person caught using a white person's water fountain would be fined.

Signs above water fountains and restrooms shouted WHITES ONLY or COLOREDS ONLY. Blacks had to make do with dirtier and older schools and bathrooms, or with parks and playgrounds covered in weeds and rust—where they existed at all. States carefully worded their Jim Crow laws so as not to offend the 14th Amendment: "Separate but equal facilities shall be available for persons of color." In reality, *separate* was rarely *equal*.

Some whites were not satisfied with laws that kept blacks from equal opportunities. Burning torches threatened black houses, farms, and businesses in the dead of night. The men who lit them wore long white robes with high, pointed white hats. Masks concealed the hatred on the faces of these white Confederate veterans, businessmen, mayors, judges, even policemen. They were the Ku Klux Klan, and they terrorized the South. The Klan burned the crops, houses, businesses,

The Ku Klux Klan began burning crosses around 1915 to strike fear into the hearts of blacks. Cross burning remains a symbol of racist violence.

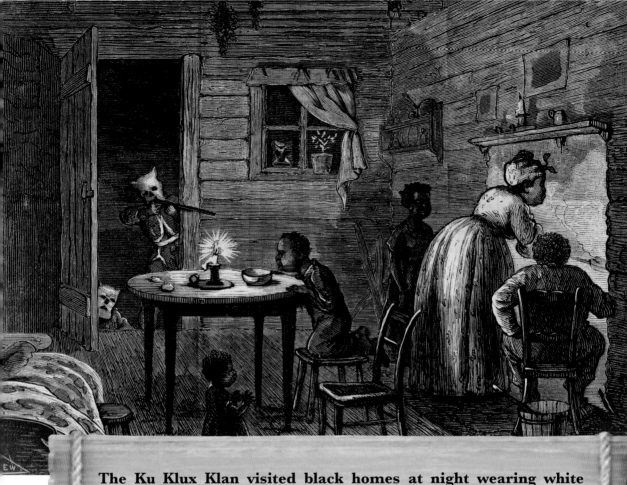

The Ku Klux Klan visited black homes at night wearing white masks and robes. They snatched black men, women, and children at gunpoint. Some blacks returned bloody and bruised, alive but afraid. Others never came home.

and bodies of black people. They carried guns to threaten, or shoot out windows, or murder blacks who got out of line. Even whites were not safe from the violence. A white person suspected of being too friendly—helping blacks get jobs or vote or, worst of all, falling in love with a black person—would feel the Klan's wrath.

Who Was Jim Crow?

Wheel about and turn about and do just so,
Every time I wheel about I jump Jim Crow.

Legend has it that popular entertainer Thomas D. Rice was hunting for a new piece to add to his act. One night after a show, he lingered at the theater stables to watch an old slave. The slave sang a song about Jim Crow. He danced in a way Rice knew his audiences would love. Rice was white, but he painted his face with dark makeup and enormous thick red lips. He wore oversized tattered clothes and shoes to look pitiful and poor. He debuted his Jim Crow act in 1828. It became an instant hit with white audiences, who soon hummed this catchy tune and tried their hand at a new dance that made slaves look happy, goofy, and stupid. By 1836, Rice's Jim Crow act had become one of the most popular songs and dances in the country.[4]

Comic strips and ads, too, cashed in on the image of blacks as clownish buffoons. In *Darktown*, a popular comic strip by Thomas Worth, clumsy black firefighters looked more like monkeys than men as they ignored a flaming house and hosed down their friends instead. Aunt Jemima—a black "mammy" housemaid who cheerfully cooked, cleaned, and cared for white families—appeared in ads selling everything from pancake mix and mayonnaise to dishwashers and detergent. These negative stereotypes reinforced racist ideas across the country.

1909 Aunt Jemima ad

CHAPTER 3

BOOKER T. AND W.E.B.

Blacks wanted opportunity, but the better neighborhoods, better schools, better jobs, and a better future were open only to whites. Segregation became a new kind of bondage, leaving blacks little hope for a better life. What could be done? Two great black leaders—Booker T. Washington and W.E.B. Du Bois—had two very different ideas.

Booker T. Washington was born in a one-room log cabin, a slave on a plantation in Franklin County, Virginia, in 1856. He and his family slept on the dirt in rags. They worked from the time they woke to the time they collapsed on the floor each night. Once slaves gained their freedom, Washington's family had little money. Young Booker worked as a house servant. His busy life left little time for fun or even sleep. But his hard work carried him through school to college.

He became a teacher so famous that President Theodore Roosevelt invited him to dinner at the White House.

Booker Taliaferro Washington believed that education and usefulness would bring success to blacks. He became the first African American to be pictured on a U.S. postage stamp (1940) or a coin (1951).

History class at Tuskegee

Energetic and tireless, 25-year-old Washington led the brand-new Tuskegee Institute in 1881. This college-level school in Tuskegee, Alabama, taught blacks the skills they needed to get useful jobs in a hands-on way.

When the institute first needed classrooms, Tuskegee students learned architecture and construction from Robert Taylor, the first black graduate of the Massachusetts Institute of Technology (M.I.T.), a famous Boston university. Tuskegee students made bricks by hand and raised walls themselves to craft the institute's buildings.

Renowned black plant biologist George Washington Carver turned the institute's land into small farms to show his students better methods of planting. The institute also trained the Tuskegee Airmen, the first black pilots, who bravely served in World War II. By the time Booker T. Washington died in 1915, the Tuskegee Institute had grown from a one-room schoolhouse to a nationally famous university of 100 buildings, teaching 1,500 students in 40 different trades.[1]

The Tuskegee Airmen

"Cast your bucket down where you are," Washington said in his famous Atlanta Compromise speech in 1895. Washington encouraged blacks to make the best of their situations.

Washington fought racism through his own example of education and hard work. He believed that if blacks everywhere also worked hard, got jobs, and became responsible citizens, then whites would open their hearts to equality for the races. But doors to the very jobs he trained his students for were often shut, simply because of the students' skin color. At the 1895 Atlanta Expo, Washington struck a bargain with whites. "In all things purely social we can be as separate as the fingers," he reassured his white audience.[2] Blacks would calmly accept segregation and Jim Crow laws, Washington said, if whites would just give them a chance to get jobs.

W.E.B. Du Bois, 1918

William Edward Burghardt (W.E.B.) Du Bois disagreed. He was born in 1868 in Massachusetts, Unlike Washington, he was a free black who went to school with white children. His white teachers urged him to go to college. They thought he would be a shoo-in at Harvard University. Instead, Harvard rejected his application because he was black. But Du Bois didn't give up. He moved to Nashville, Tennessee, to attend Fisk University. He later became Harvard's first black PhD (Doctor of Philosophy).

Du Bois studied the black population in the South as a professor at Atlanta University. Many lived in shacks or could not afford to fix their houses. Many were

unhealthy and unable to pay doctors. If Southern blacks were free, why were so many so poor?

Du Bois saw that constant fear kept most black people scared, sorrowful, and silent, afraid to dream. Gruesome lynchings—mob killings—of blacks were as common as they were horrifying. In 1899, Sam Hose, a black farmer near Atlanta, killed his white neighbor in an argument. The Ku Klux Klan murdered Hose, burned his body, and displayed what was left of him in shop windows around town as a warning to other blacks.[3] In 1916, Texas whites accused 17-year-old black Jesse Washington of murdering white Lucy Fryer. As he stood trial, a mob of angry white men stormed the courthouse. They threw a chain around the young man's neck and dragged him outside, where they tied him to a tree and set him on fire.

More than 2,500 blacks were lynched in the United States between 1884 and 1900; about 100 lynchings happened every year between 1900 and 1914.[4] Some of the black victims were accused of crimes. Others were lynched for no reason at all. Even the North was not safe for blacks. For example, in 1913, a white mob in Coatesville, Pennsylvania, killed and burned a disabled black man. Indiana boasted the largest Ku Klux Klan membership in the country.[5] Whites who murdered blacks were rarely found guilty of any crime, even when they attacked in broad daylight with many witnesses. W.E.B. Du Bois wrote in 1913, "The point is he was black. Blackness must be punished. . . . It is therefore necessary, as every white scoundrel in the nation knows, to let slip no opportunity of punishing this crime of crimes."[6]

Du Bois dedicated his life to opening the eyes of the nation

A New York City mob lynching William Jones in 1863

W.E.B. Du Bois (right) served as the NAACP's first Director of Publicity and Research. Lawyer Moorfield Storey (left) was its first president. Mary White Ovington (center), an activist for civil and women's rights, served as executive secretary.

to the real lives of blacks. In 1909, he and other black leaders created the National Association for the Advancement of Colored People (NAACP). In its official national magazine, *The Crisis,* Du Bois celebrated the achievements of black scientists and inventors. He also reported on everyday progress, such as the opening of community libraries and the growth of black neighborhoods. He used *The Crisis,* too, to rage against lynching and white riots that killed blacks.

Ida B. Wells was a fellow writer and NAACP member. Wells's friend, Tom Moss, a black businessman, ran a successful grocery store in Memphis, Tennessee. In March 1892, whites came with guns and tools and destroyed it. They lynched Moss and two of his friends, Calvin McDowell and Henry Stewart. Wells was terrified, but also furious. She knew that when the law would not stand up for justice, her mighty pen could. In her newspaper column, she urged her fellow blacks to "leave a town which will neither protect our lives and property, nor give us a fair trial in the courts, but takes us out and murders us in cold blood."[7]

Blacks took Wells's advice and packed their bags. Between 1890 and 1920, many blacks moved away from the rural Southern home of their slave ancestors in a Great Migration. Some moved to Kansas and the West in search of laws kinder to blacks. Others found new hope and homes in Northern cities like Detroit, Philadelphia, and New York. Wells moved to Chicago, where she continued to shout for justice. Together, these new black communities sowed the seeds of real change in America.

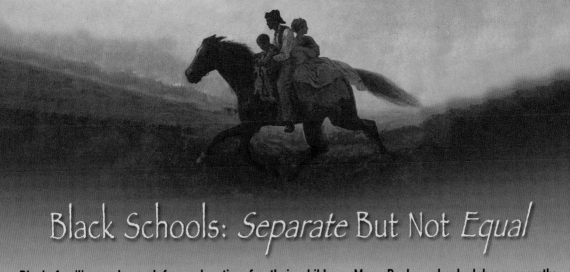

Black Schools: *Separate* But Not *Equal*

Black families welcomed free education for their children. Mary Peake, who had been secretly teaching black children for years, created the first school for blacks under a big oak tree in Hampton, Virginia, in 1861.

Black children were glad to learn, but everyone knew that black schools consistently received less funding than white schools. A black school might be only one dark room with a dirt floor. Teachers had to use outdated schoolbooks, some missing pages. There were no playgrounds, and no buses for black students. In 1900, states spent as much as ten times more on white schools than on black schools.[8] As late as 1916, only 67 black high schools existed in the entire country.[9] Laws kept blacks out of white colleges. Berea College of Kentucky had been admitting black students since 1855. In 1904, a Kentucky law declared that blacks and whites could not attend the same schools. Berea College challenged this law, but in 1908, the U.S. Supreme Court ruled against it.

Whites and blacks have attended school together now for half a century. However, studies reveal disturbing trends that show discrimination still exists in education. Schools with a greater percentage of black students were paying their teachers at least $2,000 less per year. About one in five U.S. students are black, yet over half of all fourth graders held back in 2010 were black. Black students were also over 3.5 times more likely than white students to get expelled from school.[10] Can America ever truly be equal without equal education?

Mary Peake

CHAPTER 4

THE *NEW NEGRO* FINDS A VOICE

One neighborhood blossomed right in the thick of the action of New York City. Many other cities made laws that forced blacks to live in run-down, black-only neighborhoods. In New York's Harlem, families with children lived in newer apartment buildings and well-kept homes. From this black neighborhood, a rich culture of artists grew in the 1920s and 1930s.

> *Do dah do dee do bah doo...heebah jeeb boo bah dee looby doo*

Voices like tripping, flipping trumpets spilled out into Harlem's night air as 17-year-old singer Ella Fitzgerald steamed up the Apollo Theater.

Yeah! Uh-huh! Sure! growled trumpeter Louis Armstrong from the stage at the Cotton Club, as pianists Count Basie and Jelly Roll Morton tinkled along in fast, bouncy, toe-tapping fun. Exciting new rhythms packed white audiences in for sold-out shows. They

Jazz legend
Louis Armstrong

Many modern music greats began their career performing at Harlem's Apollo Theater.

came to see and hear this new music—*jazz*. Invented and perfected by these black artists from the South, jazz became America's first original art form.

On Sunday nights, the Marshall Hotel on West 53rd Street was the scene for dinner and a show put on by famous black actors, dancers, singers, and musicians.[1] Bill "Bojangles" Robinson tap-danced his way onto the stage, up and down stairs, and later, onto the big screen with white child movie star Shirley Temple. Josephine Baker, a dancer and singer, became an international superstar in the United States and in France. Laughter bubbled out on to the street as the musical dance act of Bert Williams and George Walker performed the high-stepping cakewalk. Demand for Williams and Walker's musical comedy act took them all the way to Broadway. Their original musical *In Dahomey*, about black friends who move to Africa, became the first show to appear on Broadway that was written and performed by blacks.

Black writers found an audience not just among whites, but also among blacks who could now read and write. In 1925, Harlem scholar Alain Locke collected the writings of African Americans in his book, *The New*

Josephine Baker

Negro, to show how blacks had truly lived and felt since the Civil War. Locke's book focused on the lingering pain of slavery. While many Northern whites would rather deny that slavery had ever existed, Locke inspired Harlem's other black writers to celebrate their strength as survivors. Zora Neale Hurston used black folk stories to bring black history to life. Langston Hughes used poetry as a slow jazz in writing to speak plainly of black feelings, the black experience, and most importantly, blacks' longing to be equal. Blacks wrote of a stark life lived under the unfairness and violence of racism. But their words also spoke of everyday hopes for peace and opportunity—and freedom.

**Writer and philosopher
Alain Locke**

Zora Neale Hurston

Not everything was pitch-perfect for average blacks in cities across America. The dark-skinned "immigrants" from the South competed with immigrants from Ireland and Italy for jobs and housing. Together, these poor whites and blacks served as housekeepers for the rich, waiters at restaurants, and train porters who helped passengers. "Last ones hired, first ones fired," the disappointed blacks often said.

As a porter, Asa Philip Randolph helped train passengers on their journeys, getting them food and drinks and other things they might need. Black porters like Randolph earned a measly paycheck and no overtime. Even on long journeys, white patrons never bothered to learn their proper names. "George, will you get me a glass of water?" "George, can you help me with my heavy bag?" But blacks did not dare to complain for fear of losing their jobs.

Randolph rallied the black porters to stick together and stand up against the Pullman Company. He started a popular

Sleeping car porters were called "George" no matter what their real names were.

Advertisement for Pullman train travel

newspaper in New York City, *The Messenger*, and wrote of the unfair treatment that black workers faced every day. Randolph helped organize his fellow black porters to form the Brotherhood of Sleeping Car Porters.[2] They became the first black union, a group of workers that successfully bargained with the Pullman Company to guarantee fair pay and safe working conditions.

Encouraged by his success, Randolph realized that blacks *did* have power to change things for the better. As the United States raised an army of half a million men to send overseas, only 4,000 of them were black soldiers. The U.S. military kept trained blacks out of nearly all jobs. Randolph called blacks to action: "We

A. Philip Randolph

loyal Negro Americans demand the right to work and fight for our country!"[3]

At first, President Franklin D. Roosevelt would not listen. Randolph had an idea for a grand March on Washington in 1941. "I think we ought to get 10,000 Negroes and march down Pennsylvania Avenue asking for jobs in defense plants and integration of the armed forces. It would shake up Washington."[4] That got the President's attention. Randolph personally met with President Franklin D. Roosevelt and Vice President Harry S. Truman. He convinced them to stop all segregation in the U.S. armed forces by 1948.

In 1964, Lyndon B. Johnson awarded A. Philip Randolph the Presidential Medal of Freedom—the highest honor a U.S. civilian can receive.

Chief Justice Earl Warren (sitting center) led the U.S. Supreme Court from 1953 to 1969. The eight other justices sided with him on the desegregation of schools and many other important legal decisions. They decided that people who are arrested have rights (*Miranda v. Arizona*), and that poor defendants must have a lawyer's help in court (*Gideon v. Wainwright*).

These steps were only the beginning. Blacks continued to shout for justice. In 1954, lawyers for the NAACP presented a careful, logical case before the Supreme Court. They argued that the separate but equal decision of *Plessy v. Ferguson* made it difficult, if not impossible, for black children to receive a good education. This time, all nine justices of the Court agreed. In its *Brown v. Board of Education* decision, Chief Justice Earl Warren wrote: "separate educational facilities are inherently unequal."

The black community celebrated the news like a second emancipation. "I have seen the impossible happen," said W.E.B. Du Bois.[5] All embraced the victory, but they also wondered, *Why now and not before? What changed?*

Negro League Baseball

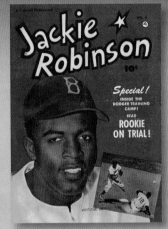

Jackie Robinson comic book

When Jackie Robinson signed his name to a contract with the Brooklyn Dodgers under manager Branch Rickey in 1947, he was not the first black person to play professional baseball. Moses and Weldon Walker, Bud Fowler, Frank Grant, and others had played in the big leagues before, even alongside whites. On the baseball field, an athlete was an athlete. But after White Sox star player Adrian "Cap" Anson refused to play on the same field as Moses Walker in July 1884, black players were blacklisted.[6] They were not allowed in the minors, and without experience in the minors, they could never make the majors.

Negro leagues sprouted up all across the country. Fans wanted to see Josh Gibson. He had a lifetime batting average of .423 and nearly 800 home runs over his 17-year career. (His white fans called Babe Ruth the "white Josh Gibson.") Legendary pitcher Satchel Paige set strikeout records with the Chattanooga Black Lookouts. Hall-of-famer Hank Aaron also got his start for the Mobile Black Bears, swatting his Indianapolis Clowns into the 1952 Negro League championships.

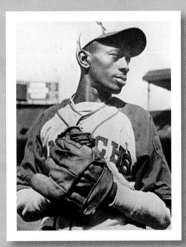

Satchel Paige

Black history took a major turn in 1947. Jackie Robinson became the first black to play for modern Major League Baseball (MLB). In Robinson's first game, pitchers threw fastballs at his head. Runners stepped on him. Players even threatened his family. Robinson just kept playing, winning more fans each day and taking home the trophy for Rookie of the Year. In 1949, he was named MLB's Most Valuable Player.

CHAPTER 5

THE MARCH TO FREEDOM

While strides were made in the courtroom, racism endured throughout the country. Newspapers, radio, and TV gave Americans a new view of the ugly reality of racism. On August 28, 1955, Emmett Till's mother held a public funeral, insisting that newspapers show Emmett's mangled body to the world. Fifteen-year-old Emmett had been visiting his uncle in Mississippi when two white men kidnapped the black boy. They beat him, gouged out one of his eyes, shot him, and dumped him in the Tallahatchie River. Shouting from front-page headlines, the horrors that terrorized black people every day could no longer be ignored.

On November 14, 1960, TV audiences watched as six-year-old Ruby Bridges walked up the steps of William Frantz Elementary School in New Orleans. Little Ruby became the first black student to integrate into a white school. But what could have been a proud moment for America turned hateful. An angry white mob yelled and threw things

U.S. Marshals stood by Ruby Bridges to protect her from the many death threats she received on her first day at the all-white William Frantz Elementary school. White parents kept their kids home from school, so Ruby and her white teacher, Barbara Henry, spent the kindergarten year alone in the classroom.

Rosa Parks and Martin Luther King, Jr.

at the girl. One woman held up a black baby doll in a coffin. Armed guards and several U.S. Marshals were called in to protect this child.

While many whites were finally waking up to the message, blacks realized they could use TV and radio as a peaceful way to come together and show their strength. They had already begun this movement with a bus ride in Alabama.

It rained on December 1, 1955. Forty-two-year-old Rosa Parks sat in the black section of the crowded bus. Soon the white section filled up, leaving nowhere for a new passenger to sit. Driver James Blake turned.

"Let me have those seats."

He expected the black folks to get up and stand, to make room for the white man to sit down. Three black passengers did get up, but not Rosa. She was tired of giving in.

Furious, Blake stormed to her seat, screaming, "Are you gonna get up?"

"No."

"I'm going to have you arrested!"

"You may go on and do so."

Martin Luther King, Jr.

After Rosa Parks sat down, blacks everywhere stood up. TV and radio coverage of Rosa's story made it clear to many others—they didn't have to put up with the unfair rules. Blacks, and a few whites, protested in the Montgomery Bus Boycott. Nearly 75 percent of National City Lines' usual customers refused to ride the buses in Montgomery, choosing to walk instead.[1]

With peaceful action and strength in numbers, blacks had won. Martin Luther King, Jr. helped organize the boycott. He drove carpools and urged protesters to stay calm. "We must love our white brothers, no matter what they do to us," the young preacher told them. Whites firebombed King's house, but still he urged, "This is what we must live by, we must meet hate with love."[2]

After 381 days, the nearly bankrupt bus company agreed to change the rules. No longer would there be separate sections for whites and blacks. All would ride equally.

Not everyone believed that peace was the way to go. When Malcolm X was a boy, the Ku Klux Klan burned down his family's house and murdered his father. "There's no such thing as a nonviolent revolution," Malcolm often proclaimed.

Was Malcolm X right? Harry and Harriette Moore, teachers and civil rights

Malcolm X

leaders in Florida, were killed when the Ku Klux Klan bombed their house in 1951. A white racist gunned down the activist Medgar Evers in his own driveway in Mississippi in 1963. As blacks held marches and boycotts, standing up to injustice with sit-ins and other nonviolent protests, police beat them with fists or clubs, or they sent in dogs to attack. But the protesters did not stop. And as the movement grew, more whites joined them.

On August 28, 1963, more than 200,000 people gathered for the March on Washington for Jobs and Freedom. People of every skin color from all across the United States walked together from the Washington Monument to the steps of the Lincoln Memorial. A. Philip Randolph himself stood before them, his long-time dream a reality. "Let the nation and the world know the meaning of our numbers," he proclaimed. This is "a new beginning not only for the Negro but for all Americans who thirst for freedom and a better life."[3]

President John F. Kennedy met with the leaders that day, pledging to turn their efforts into law. On January 23, 1964, the 24th Amendment to the Constitution outlawed poll taxes that prevented poor people, especially blacks, from voting. On July 2, the Civil Rights Act of 1964 passed, making discrimination illegal. No

Leaders of the March on Washington joined President John F. Kennedy (center) and members of his Cabinet in the Oval Office on August 28, 1963.

more could blacks be shoved off to separate but unequal schools. No more would blacks be subject to strange and unusual laws that made it difficult for them to vote, attend schools, obtain jobs, or serve in the military.

But in 1965, as civil rights workers tried to register black voters in Alabama, police attacked with tear gas and clubs. A white state trooper shot and killed black preacher Jimmie Lee Jackson as he helped voters that February. Determined to make a stand, over 2,900 people marched together from Selma, Alabama, to the state capitol of Montgomery. Whites and blacks linked arms or walked hand in hand. Their 54-mile journey took three days. By day, Alabama racists jeered and threw trash at them. Police attacked, first with clubs, then with dogs. By night, friendly farmers let the tired marchers rest in their fields.

Blacks and whites together carry American flags and march peacefully through Alabama towns, past homes and the E.A. Drinkard Grocery Store.

President Lyndon B. Johnson shakes hands with Martin Luther King, Jr. and other black leaders.

Washington, D.C., heard their protest. On August 6, 1965, almost 100 years to the day after the first Juneteenth, President Lyndon B. Johnson signed the 1965 Voter Rights Act into law. No more could anyone try to stop blacks or any other race from having their say in America's future.

Today, civil rights laws protect a blended nation, giving all Americans the right to pursue their dreams. Blacks and whites live and work together in every corner of America. The deepest dreams of many African Americans came true with the election of President Barack Obama in 2008. "It's been a long time coming," Obama said in his victory speech, "but change has come to America."[4]

Progress does not mean perfection. Time and again, civil rights laws have been tested by fear, pride, and stubbornness.

In 2015, videos on YouTube made national news, accusing U.S. police of treating blacks unfairly. Protests erupted in New York, Baltimore, Detroit, and Chicago in response. Some demonstrations were peaceful. Others turned to riots that destroyed entire neighborhoods. Time and again, the issue of civil rights has been challenged. While much progress has been made, much more needs to be done to ensure that everyone is truly equal under the law.

Deadly Discrimination?

Several cases of deadly police action have been noted for spurring the 2015 racial protests.

On July 17, 2014, Eric Garner insisted he was not selling single cigarettes out of a pack (which is illegal). Still, white New York City police officer Daniel Pantaleo took him down. He shoved the 44-year-old black man's face and neck into the street. Garner died from his injuries.

On August 9, 2014, video footage showed Michael Brown stealing cigarettes from a store in Ferguson, Missouri. When white officer Darren Wilson caught up to him, the two struggled. Wilson fired 12 shots that killed the unarmed black teen.

On April 4, 2015, Walter Scott, a 50-year-old black man, was pulled over in North Carolina. His car's brake light was not working properly. However, there was a warrant out for Scott's arrest—he owed child support payments. He ran from white officer Michael Slager. Slager shot Scott five times in the back, killing him with a bullet to the heart. Scott was unarmed.

Freddie Gray

One week later, Baltimore police arrested Freddie Gray, a 25-year-old black man with a history of drug-related arrests. This time, an officer thought Gray had an illegal switchblade. Gray was cuffed and dragged to a police van. On the way to the police station, Gray collapsed in a coma. He died a few days later from spinal injuries.

1619	Slavery in America begins when the first African slaves are brought to Jamestown, Virginia, to work on tobacco plantations.
1663	The first recorded slave rebellion takes place in Gloucester County, Virginia.
1738	Fugitive slaves establish Fort Mose in Florida. It is the first permanent African-American settlement in America.
1793	The U.S. Congress passes the first Fugitive Slave Law.
1820	The Missouri Compromise allows Missouri to enter the Union as a slave state, but makes slavery illegal in Maine. It prohibits slavery above the 36° 30´ latitude line in the rest of the Louisiana Territory.
1850	The Fugitive Slave Law is passed, making it illegal to help runaways in any manner.
1854	The Kansas-Nebraska Act repeals the Missouri Compromise.
1857	In the Dred Scott Decision, the U.S. Supreme Court rules that slaves are not considered citizens under the U.S. Constitution but are the property of their owners.
1861	The Civil War begins.
1863	On January 1, Abraham Lincoln's Emancipation Proclamation frees slaves in the Confederate States.
1865	The Civil War ends. The 13th Amendment abolishes slavery throughout the United States. Texas hears the news on June 16, a holiday still celebrated as Juneteenth.
1866	Congress creates the black regiments the 9th and 10th Cavalry and the 24th and 25th Infantry. These "Buffalo Soldiers" patrol the western frontier and serve as rangers in national parks. They also serve in several wars until the U.S. army integrates the troops.
1868	The 14th Amendment grants citizenship to "all persons born or naturalized in the United States," including former slaves.
1870	The 15th Amendment grants African-American men the right to vote.
1884	Black baseball players were banned from the minor leagues.
1890	The Great Migration begins, African Americans move north and west from the South.
1896	In *Plessy v. Ferguson,* the U.S. Supreme Court declares "separate but equal" to be legal.
1909	The National Association for the Advancement of Colored People (NAACP) is founded.
1920s	Black culture and arts flourish in New York during the Harlem Renaissance.
1947	Jackie Robinson is the first black player to sign a contract with Major League Baseball.
1948	The U.S. armed forces are no longer segregated.
1954	The U.S. Supreme Court overturns the *Plessy* decision in *Brown v. Board of Education,* saying separate schools are not equal, and therefore are illegal.
1955	Martin Luther King, Jr. organizes the Montgomery Bus Boycott. It lasts 381 days.
1964	The 24th Amendment outlaws poll taxes. The Civil Rights Act, which integrates schools and other public places and forbids race discrimination at the workplace.
2001	*International Underground Railroad Memorial* is placed in Detroit, Michigan, and Canada.
2014	African-American Michael Brown is shot by a white police officer in Ferguson, Missouri, sparking racial tensions.
2015	Rioting continues across the United States after the U.S. Department of Justice reports on evidence of racial profiling in law enforcement in Ferguson, Missouri.

Chapter 1. Free at Last!

1. Henry Louis Gates, Jr. and Donald Yacovone, *The African Americans: Many Rivers to Cross* (Los Angeles: Smiley Books, 2013), p. 128.

2. Manning Marable and Leith Mullings, *Freedom: A Photographic History of the African-American Struggle* (New York: Phaidon Press, 2002), p. 15.

3. Ibid.

4. Tonya Bolden, *Cause: Reconstruction America, 1863–1877* (New York: Alfred A. Knopf, 2005), p. 31.

5. Ibid., p. 26.

6. John Hope Franklin and Alfred A. Moss, Jr., *From Slavery to Freedom: A History of Negro Americans,* 6th Ed. (New York: McGraw-Hill, Inc., 1988), pp. 137–138.

7. Julius Lester, *To Be a Slave* (New York: Dial Books, 1998), pp. 146–147.

Chapter 2. Whites Only, Coloreds Only

1. Alex McBride, "Landmark Cases: Plessy v. Ferguson (1896)," *The Supreme Court,* PBS, 2006, http://www.pbs.org/wnet/supremecourt/antebellum/landmark_plessy.html

2. Ibid.

3. "Examples of Jim Crow Laws," *The Jackson Sun,* 2001, http://www.ferris.edu/jimcrow/links/misclink/examples/homepage.htm

4. "Jim Crow," *Africans in America,* PBS, 2000, http://www.pbs.org/wgbh/aia/part3/3h489.html

Chapter 3. Booker T. and W.E.B.

1. Tuskegee University, www.tuskegee.edu.

2. Booker T. Washington, *Up from Slavery* (New York: Tribeca Books, 2013), p. 107.

3. David L. Lewis, *W.E.B. Du Bois: A Biography* (New York: Macmillan, 2009), p. 162.

4. John Hope Franklin and Alfred A. Moss, Jr., *From Slavery to Freedom: A History of Negro Americans,* 6th Ed. (New York: McGraw-Hill, Inc., 1988), p. 282.

5. Manning Marable and Leith Mullings, *Freedom: A Photographic History of the African-American Struggle* (New York: Phaidon Press, 2002), p. 132.

6. David L. Lewis, *W.E.B. Du Bois: A Biography* (New York: Macmillan, 2009), p. 280.

7. Henry Louis Gates, Jr. and Donald Yacovone, *The African Americans: Many Rivers to Cross* (Los Angeles: Smiley Books, 2013), p. 155.

8. Franklin and Moss, p. 243.

9. Marable and Mullings, p. 38.

10. Caralee J. Adams, Erik W. Robelen, and Nirvi Shah, "Civil Rights Data Show Retention Disparities," *Education Week,* March 6, 2012.

Chapter 4. The *New Negro* Finds a Voice

1. Jennifer Fronc, "The Marshall Hotel," Gotham Center for New York City History. http://www.gothamcenter.org/blotter/?p=377

2. John Hope Franklin and Alfred A. Moss, Jr., *From Slavery to Freedom: A History of Negro Americans,* 6th Ed. (New York: McGraw-Hill, Inc., 1988), p. 340.

3. The White House Historical Association, "FDR, A. Philip Randolph and the Desegregation of the Defense Industries," http://www.whitehousehistory.org/whha_classroom/classroom_9-12-pressure-defense.html

4. Ibid.

5. Henry Louis Gates, Jr. and Donald Yacovone, *The African Americans: Many Rivers to Cross* (Los Angeles: Smiley Books, 2013), p. 217.

6. Steven Goldman, "Segregated Baseball: A Kaleidoscopic Review," MLB.com.

Chapter 5. The March to Freedom

1. Henry Louis Gates, Jr. and Donald Yacovone, *The African Americans: Many Rivers to Cross* (Los Angeles: Smiley Books, 2013), p. 221.

2. Roger Bruns, *Martin Luther King, Jr.: A Biography* (Westport, CT: Greenwood Publishing Group, 2006), p. 42.

3. "For Jobs and Freedom: The Leaders Speak," *The Crisis,* August–September 1973, Vol. 80, No 7., p. 228.

4. "Sen. Barack Obama's Acceptance Speech in Chicago, Ill.," *The Washington Post,* November 5, 2008.

Malcolm X

Adams, Caralee J., Erik W. Robelen, and Nirvi Shah. "Civil Rights Data Show Retention Disparities." *Education Week,* March 6, 2012.

Alexander, Michelle. *The New Jim Crow.* New York: The New Press, 2012.

Altmas, Susan. *The Encyclopedia of African-American Heritage.* New York: Facts on File, 1997.

Bolden, Tonya. *Cause: Reconstruction America, 1863–1877.* New York: Alfred A. Knopf, 2005.

Brands, H.W. *American Colossus: The Triumph of Capitalism 1865–1900.* New York: Doubleday, 2010.

Bruns, Roger. *Martin Luther King, Jr.: A Biography.* Westport, CT: Greenwood Publishing Group, 2006.

Chafe, William H. *The Rise and Fall of the American Century: The United States from 1890 to 2009.* New York: Oxford University Press, 2009.

"Examples of Jim Crow Laws." *The Jackson Sun,* 2001. http://www.ferris.edu/jimcrow/links/misclink/examples/homepage.htm

Ferris State University: The Jim Crow Museum of Racist Memorabilia. http://www.ferris.edu/jimcrow/

"For Jobs and Freedom: The Leaders Speak," *The Crisis,* August-September 1973, Vol. 80, No. 7., p. 228.

Franklin, John Hope, and Alfred A. Moss, Jr. *From Slavery to Freedom: A History of Negro Americans.* 6th Ed. New York: McGraw-Hill, Inc., 1988.

Fronc, Jennifer. "The Marshall Hotel." Gotham Center for New York City History, http://www.gothamcenter.org/blotter/?p=377

Gates, Jr., Henry Louis, and Donald Yacovone. *The African Americans: Many Rivers to Cross.* Los Angeles: Smiley Books, 2013.

Goldman, Steven. "Segregated Baseball: A Kaleidoscopic Review." *MLB.com.*

"Jim Crow." *Africans in America.* PBS. 2000. http://www.pbs.org/wgbh/aia/part3/3h489.html

Lester, Julius. *To Be a Slave.* New York: Dial Books, 1998.

Lewis, David L. *W.E.B. Du Bois: A Biography.* New York: Macmillan, 2009.

Marable, Manning, and Leith Mullings. *Freedom: A Photographic History of the African-American Struggle.* New York: Phaidon Press, 2002.

McBride, Alex. "Landmark Cases: Plessy v. Ferguson (1896)." *The Supreme Court.* PBS, 2006. http://www.pbs.org/wnet/supremecourt/antebellum/landmark_plessy.html

"The Rise and Fall of Jim Crow." PBS. http://www.pbs.org/wnet/jimcrow/

"Sen. Barack Obama's Acceptance Speech in Chicago, Ill.," *The Washington Post,* November 5, 2008.

Steptoe, Gabriel Burns. *The African American Years: Chronologies of American History and Experience.* New York: Charles Scribner's Sons, 2003.

Tuskegee University. http://www.tuskegee.edu.

Washington, Booker T. *Up from Slavery.* New York: Tribeca Books, 2013.

The White House Historical Association. "FDR, A. Philip Randolph and the Desegregation of the Defense Industries." http://www.whitehousehistory.org/whha_classroom/classroom_9-12-pressure-defense.html

Books

Abdul-Jabbar, Kareem, and Raymond Obstfeld. *What Color Is My World?: The Lost History of African-American Inventors.* Somerville, Massachusetts: Candlewick Press, 2012.

Curtis, Christopher Paul. *The Watsons Go to Birmingham—1963.* New York: Random House, 2013.

Hakim, Joy. *Reconstructing America: 1865–1890.* New York: Oxford University Press, 2003.

Muldoon, Kathleen. *The Jim Crow Era.* Edina, Minnesota: ABDO Publishing, 2014.

Nelson, Kadir. *Heart and Soul: The Story of America and African-Americans.* New York: Balzer + Bray, 2011.

Nelson, Kadir. *We Are The Ship: The Story of Negro League Baseball.* New York: Disney, 2008.

Pinkney, Andrea Davis. *Hand in Hand: Ten Black Men Who Changed America.* New York: Disney, 2012.

Poetry for Young People: Langston Hughes. Ed. David Roessel and Arnold Rampersad. New York: Sterling Children's Books, 2013.

Williams-Garcia, Rita. *One Crazy Summer.* New York: HarperCollins, 2010.

Woodson, Jacqueline. *Brown Girl Dreaming.* New York: Penguin Group, 2014.

On the Internet

Indianapolis Public Library Kids' Blog—"Homework: Black History Month"
http://www.imcpl.org/kids/blog/?page_id=12747

Juneteenth World Wide Celebration
http://www.juneteenth.com

National Museum of African American History and Culture
http://nmaahc.si.edu

PBS: African American World for Kids
http://pbskids.org/aaworld/

Scholastic Kids Press Corps: Black History
http://www.scholastic.com/browse/collection.jsp?id=706

Time for Kids: "Black History Month"
http://www.timeforkids.com/minisite/black-history-month

blacklist—A list of people who are not to be given certain jobs as punishment.

boycott (BOY-kot)—To refuse to buy something or use a service in the hopes of bringing social or political change.

civil rights (SIV-ul RITES)—Equal rights for all people, guaranteed by citizenship.

discrimination (dis-krih-mih-NAY-shun)—Treating someone or something differently because of the group or class to which he, she, or it belongs.

integration (in-teh-GRAY-shun)—Combining previously separate groups into a single group.

Jim Crow—A set of laws that set blacks apart from whites.

lynch (LINCH)—To murder by mob violence, without a proper trial.

martial law (MAR-shul LAW)—Using police action to keep a society in order.

poll tax (POHL TAX)—A fee that must be paid in order to vote.

porter (POR-tur)—A railroad attendant.

prejudice (PREH-joo-dis)—An opinion or feeling made without facts or understanding.

racism (RAYS-izm)—Hating other people based on their skin color or beliefs.

Reconstruction (ree-kon-STRUK-shun)—A period of American history (1865–1877) immediately following the Civil War when the states that had left the Union were admitted back into the Union and reorganized.

Renaissance (REH-nuh-zonts)—A period of great and important gains, especially in art, literature, and knowledge.

segregation (seh-greh-GAY-shun)—Setting two groups apart from each other.

sharecropping (SHAYR-krop-ing)—Farming on rented land, with the farmer allowed to keep a share of the owner's profits.

stereotype (STAYR-ee-oh-typ)—To assume an individual has certain characteristics based on the person's race or religion and not based on facts about the person.

union (YOON-yun)—A group of workers that bargains with a company for better pay and working conditions.